THE LENTEN SKETCHES

by Joseph M. Martin
Orchestration by Brant Adams

CONTENTS

3   **Portrait of Grace**

14   **Behold, the King of Zion Comes**

23   **From an Upper Room**

35   **Scenes from Gethsemane**

45   **Tableau of Sorrow**

55   **Pietà**

68   **Epilogue**

(1) This symbol indicates a track number on the Studiotrax CD (Accompaniment Only).

A DIVISION OF SHAWNEE PRESS, INC.
EXCLUSIVELY DISTRIBUTED BY HAL LEONARD CORPORATION

Copyright © 2009 HAL LEONARD – MILWIN MUSIC CORP. and HAL LEONARD CORPORATION
International Copyright Secured   All Rights Reserved

Visit Shawnee Press Online at
www.shawneepress.com

FOREWORD

Inspired by the life and message of Jesus Christ, artists in every medium have endeavored to capture the magnificence of His ministry among us. From poets and painters to singers and sculptors, the human spirit has long labored to convey through artistic expression the deep, deep things of faith. So vast is this great mystery that no canvas can capture it and no song can fully express its beauty and emotion.

As we gather together to reflect and pray, may our art be redeemed by divine purpose and our music motivated by the spirit of worship. May we offer our simple gifts of sound and sight as a testimony to the faith we long to honor and share. May we cradle in our humble frames the work of the Master Artist and may the chapels of our hearts display His beautiful portrait of grace.

Joseph M. Martin

PROGRAM NOTES

For many years I have wanted to do a cantata based on works of sacred art. There are so many splendid examples through the ages that chronicle the important moments of our faith that one hardly knows where to begin. In "The Lenten Sketches" I have chosen to focus on some of the important scenes in the last days of Christ's life, and with words and music build a frame to cradle God's Masterpiece of grace. You may wish to display examples of a variety of artist's works dealing with the various tableaus of the Passion. These can be displayed around the auditorium or in the narthex of the church for people to contemplate before entering the sanctuary. Utilizing new technology to display examples of art during each movement can be explored when appropriate. THE DIGITAL RESOURCE KIT also offers suggestions for creative movement and other innovative presentation options.

On page 67 there are two options for concluding the service following the singing of *Pietà*.

PORTRAIT OF GRACE

Words and music by
JOSEPH M. MARTIN (BMI)

3

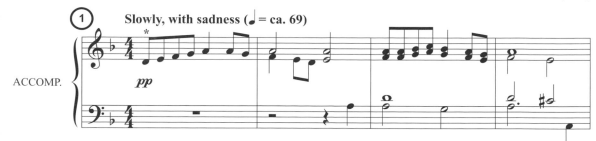

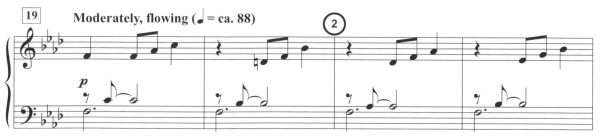

* Tune: PICARDY, French melody, 17th century

Copyright © 2009 by HAL LEONARD - MILWIN MUSIC CORP.
International Copyright Secured. All Rights Reserved.

**Duplication of this publication is illegal, and duplication is not granted
by the CCLI, LicenSing or OneLicense.net licenses.**

Come wea - ry pil - grim, kneel and re - mem - ber,

rest in the si - lence of this sa - cred place.

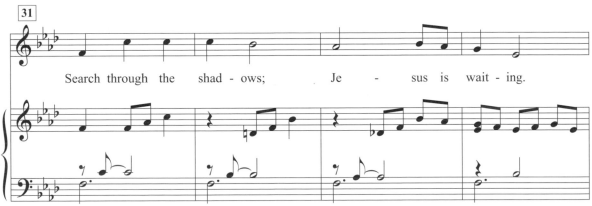

Search through the shad - ows; Je - sus is wait - ing.

See in His pas - sion a por - trait of grace. O

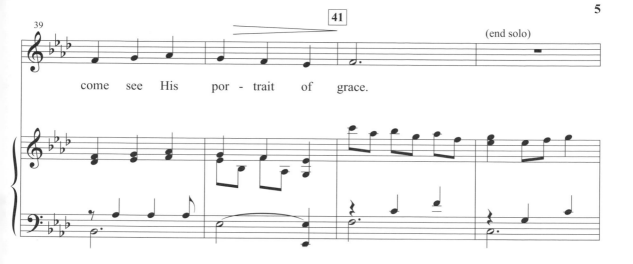

come see His por - trait of grace.

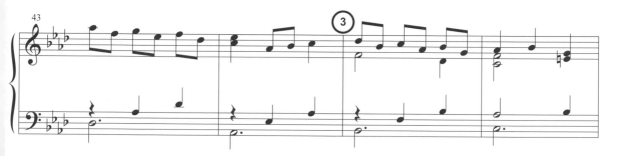

Loo_____

Come to the gar - den, kneel and re - mem - ber.

6

See neath the ol - ives the Son of God prays.

Look through the shad - ows, Jesus is weep - ing.
Loo Jesus is weep - ing.

See in His pas - sion a por - trait of grace. O

Come, come, kneel and re -

mem - ber. Weep for the Sav - ior who dies in our

place._____ Mi - se - re - re,

unis. cresc. poco a poco

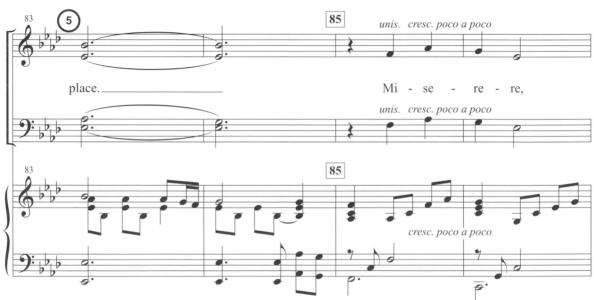

cresc. poco a poco

PORTRAIT OF GRACE - SATB

Jesus stood above the great city and wept. Through the morning mist He could see the ancient gates of Jerusalem. In the stillness of the moment He remembered the prophets who had gone before Him. Throughout the centuries their noble words of promise called out again and again, but they were all too often drowned out by the noise of hatred and violence.

Like a parent longing for a wandering child, His spirit ached to gather the people safely to His side. Like a faithful Shepherd caring for his flock, He wanted to hold them close to His heart and shelter them in His arms of grace.

The sun rose higher in the sky and the road to Jerusalem stretched out before Him. He began to walk – fully knowing the path ahead was paved with sorrow, but such was the power of His great love for the people. He must go to them and speak the words of promise again. The truth must once again ring through the winding streets of the city.

Through His tears of compassion He saw large crowds of people coming to meet Him. They were waving palms and shouting praises. The people for a moment had seen a great light and they rushed to welcome their promised King.

BEHOLD, THE KING OF ZION COMES

Words by
JOSEPH M. MARTIN

Music by
JOSEPH M. MARTIN (BMI)
Based on tune: **MORNING SONG**
from "Repository of Sacred Music, Part Second"

Be - hold, the King__ of Zi - on comes, the

Copyright © 2009 by HAL LEONARD - MILWIN MUSIC CORP.
International Copyright Secured. All Rights Reserved.

Duplication of this publication is illegal, and duplication is not granted
by the CCLI, LicenSing or OneLicense.net licenses.

prom - ise is ful - filled. The___ vi - sions seen by

proph - et eyes, to all is now,___ in truth, re - vealed, to

all___ is now___ re - vealed. From

nigh. Ho - san - na, ho - san - na! Ho -

nigh.

san - na to the King! O bless-ed is He! O

bless - ed is He who comes in the name of the

an - cient doors. Fling o - pen wide, ye gates.___

O - pen ye gates neath chap - els made___ of palms,___ and praise. Your

King___ rides hum - bly on to___ reign. Your King___ rides on___ to

Flickering candles cast long shadows upon the walls of the upper room as Jesus gathered with the disciples for the Passover feast. In this humble sanctuary the King of kings, the Creator of all life, knelt before His creation and washed the feet of His followers. Becoming a servant, the Son of God displayed the true nature of love as He comforted His friends. *[music begins]*

[begin measure 6, beat 3]
As it grew time for the Passover meal to be served, Jesus shared with His chosen ones the very heart of His mission. "This is my body given for you." The disciples watched in wonder as the Savior lifted a chalice of wine. "This is my blood, the blood of the new covenant shed for the redemption of many."

It was there, in a simple room made of stone, that a new portrait of grace was given to the world.

FROM AN UPPER ROOM

Words and music by
JOSEPH M. MARTIN (BMI)

* Tune: PICARDY, French melody, 17th century

Copyright © 2009 by HAL LEONARD - MILWIN MUSIC CORP.
International Copyright Secured. All Rights Reserved.

Duplication of this publication is illegal, and duplication is not granted
by the CCLI, LicenSing or OneLicense.net licenses.

17 **Flowing steadily** ($\bullet\cdot$ = ca. 88)

SOPRANO

mp unis.

ALTO

On the night He was be - trayed,

TENOR

mp unis.

BASS

Je - sus took the bread and wine. Gath - ered with the

drink this wine. It is my

blood, shed for you.

In a shad - owed up - per room, in that hum - ble

bo - dy. Come and drink this wine.

It is my blood, shed for you.

* King of kings, yet born of ____

* Words: From the *Liturgy of St. James,* 5th century
  tr. Gerald Moultrie (1829-1885), alt.

FROM AN UPPER ROOM - SATB

Ma - ry, as of old on earth He_____ stood.

Lord of lords in hu - man_____ ves - ture, in the bo - dy and the_____

blood, He will give to all the faith - ful, His own blood for heav'n - ly food.

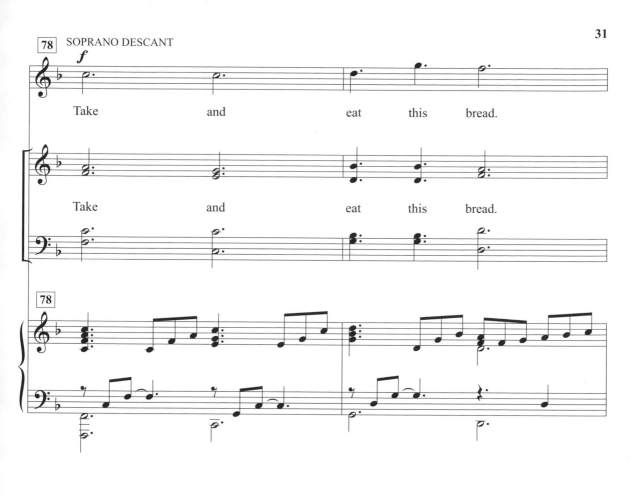

(end descant)

Come and drink this wine.

Come and drink this wine.

This is my blood._____ This is my

love._____ This is my life

giv - en for you._____

Gethsemane was a special place of quiet and solitude for Jesus. He would often go there to pray and be silent among the beauty of His creation. Following the Passover meal Jesus and the disciples once again walked through the gates of the garden. Seeking comfort and refuge they quieted themselves beneath a canopy of olive trees.

The sylvan shadows of the grove crept across the ground as the evening grew deep. With the night falling hard about them, the disciples fell asleep while Jesus fell to the ground in agony. "Father, take this cup from me," He cried into the silent night. "If there be another way, take from me this bitter wine." His tearful cry rang out across the valley in lonesome echoes of sorrow and pain. As the earth caught His sweat drops of blood, Jesus surrendered His heart to the Father's will and embraced His calling.

Suddenly the golden stars shining in the distance became torches of violence. Led by Judas, armed Centurions burst into the sanctuary of the garden looking for Jesus.

"Father, let Thy will be done," He spoke as He rose to face His destiny.

in loving memory of Melvina Jones

SCENES FROM GETHSEMANE

Words by
J. PAUL WILLIAMS (ASCAP)

Music by
JOSEPH M. MARTIN (BMI)

Available separately: 35019141

Copyright © 1997 by Harold Flammer Music and Malcolm Music, divisions of Shawnee Press, Inc.
International Copyright Secured. All Rights Reserved.

**Duplication of this publication is illegal, and duplication is not granted
by the CCLI, LicenSing or OneLicense.net licenses.**

36

Hear the Sav- ior as He grieves.

Fa - ther, Fa - ther, let this cup pass by

me. Fa - ther, Fa - ther,

Jesus was brought into in the Praetorium and stood before Pontius Pilate the Roman governor. Though Pilate could find no just reason to detain Jesus, he acquiesced to the frenzied cries of the gathering mob and gave Jesus over to be executed.

Taken from the courts Jesus was beaten and then forced to carry a heavy wooden cross up a winding path to the place known as Golgotha, "the place of the skull." There, outside the city walls, Christ's battered body was nailed to crude timbers and raised into place. A strange stillness blanketed the land as the Lamb of God began to die.
[music begins]

[begin measure 3]
With outstretched arms the Savior embraced the world with an everlasting love. With each whispered word He proclaimed forgiveness and kindness. Unbounded grace flowed from His heart and baptized the barren soil around the cross with scarlet promise. "Father forgive them," He cried into the shadows. The heavens echoed in reply with rolls of living thunder.

Standing like a mighty tower of strength, the cross reconciled heaven and earth once again. The ancient wounds were healed and the scars of sin were banished forever. For it is written, "Surely He has borne our griefs and carried our sorrows. He was wounded for our transgressions, and with His stripes we are healed."

TABLEAU OF SORROW

Words by
JOSEPH M. MARTIN
Inspired by a text by
JOHN ELLERTON (1826-1893)

Music by
JOSEPH M. MARTIN (BMI)
Incorporating tune:
HERZLIEBSTER JESU
by **JOHANN CRÜGER (1598-1662)**

Freely, with expression (♩ = ca. 69)

ACCOMP.

* Tune: PICARDY, French melody, 17th century

Copyright © 2009 by HAL LEONARD - MILWIN MUSIC CORP.
International Copyright Secured. All Rights Reserved.

Duplication of this publication is illegal, and duplication is not granted
by the CCLI, LicenSing or OneLicense.net licenses.

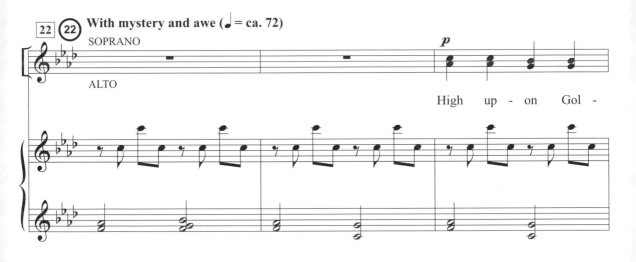

With mystery and awe (♩ = ca. 72)

SOPRANO

ALTO

High up - on Gol -

go - tha's tree, Je - sus moans in ag - o - ny.

Darkness falls a-cross His face. Shad-ows crush His

heart of grace. Who can tell what love un-known___

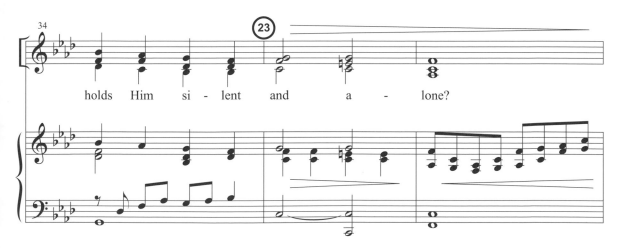

holds Him si-lent and a-lone?

Christ, God's own a- noint - ed one.

You are ask - ing, can it be? "Why have you for -

sak - en me?"

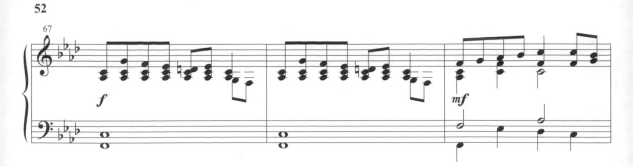

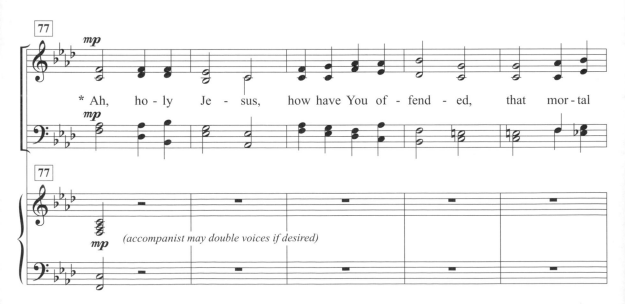

* Ah, ho - ly Je - sus, how have You of - fend - ed, that mor - tal

(accompanist may double voices if desired)

* Tune: HERZLIEBSTER JESUS, Johann Crüger (1598-1662)
Words: Johann Heermann (1585-1647), tr. Robert Bridges (1844-1930), alt.

TABLEAU OF SORROW - SATB

judg - ment has on__ You de - scend - ed? By foes de -

rid - ed, by Your own re - ject - ed, Lamb__ most af -

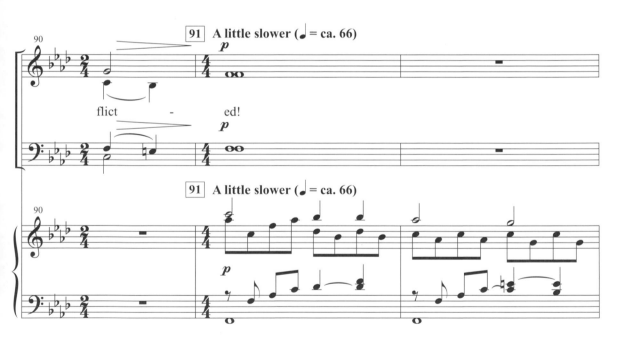

flict - ed!

91 A little slower (♩ = ca. 66)

p

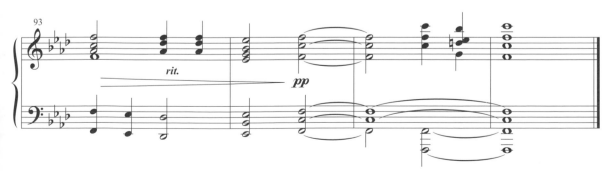

As Jesus hung in the cruel embrace of a cross, He reached out to
His mother with great tenderness and love. Even as He was covered
with the sorrows and grief of a sinful world, His heart broke for Mary's
sadness. In His compassion He asked John to care for her.

As Mary watched her son's life ebb away, she remembered all the
miracles and wonders of His incredible life. She remembered the day
the angel spoke to her and how her fear was turned to joy. She could
remember that evening in the Bethlehem stable when she gazed into His
beautiful eyes and sang a mother's first lullaby. She can still see Him
running down the path as a young boy. "Look how tall He has become!
He'll be a man in just no time at all!" she told Joseph.

She remembered dreaming about His future, this miracle son. "When
you are grown... you'll lay your hands to wood just like your Father,"
she remembered telling Him. *[music begins]*

[begin measure 1, end measure 7]
Suddenly her reverie is broken. "It is finished!" He cried from the
cross. "Father into your care I commend my Spirit." Overwhelmed by
grief, she looked into His eyes one last time as they closed in death.

[begin measure 9]
After they took Jesus down from the cross, she held Him a final time
and washed His wounds with her tears.

commissioned by Penny Dixon, Director of Music at First Evangelical Lutheran Church
in Idaho Falls, Idaho, in thanksgiving to God for her 35 years of music ministry

PIETÀ

Words and music by
JOSEPH M. MARTIN (BMI)

* Tune: PICARDY, French melody, 17th century
** Part for Violin (or other C-Instrument) is on pages 71-72.
Available separately - 35016992

Copyright © 2005, 2009 by HAL LEONARD - MILWIN MUSIC CORP.
International Copyright Secured. All Rights Reserved.

Duplication of this publication is illegal, and duplication is not granted
by the CCLI, LicenSing or OneLicense.net licenses.

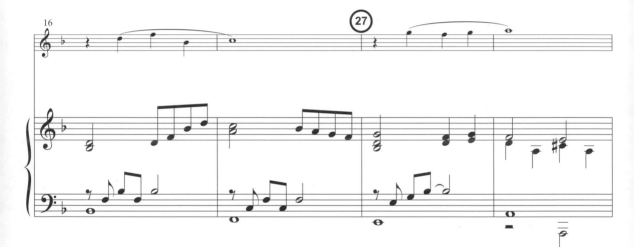

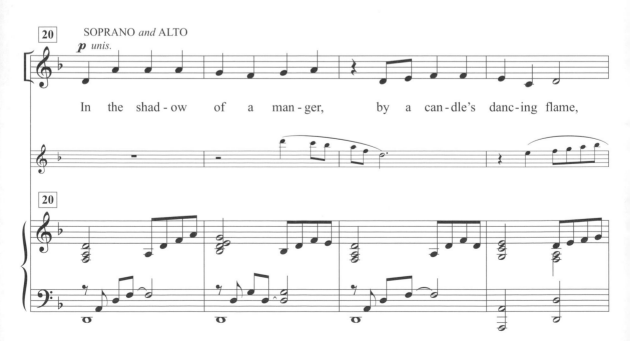

In the shad - ow of a man - ger, by a can - dle's danc - ing flame,

SOPRANO *and* ALTO
p unis.

ten - der Ma - ry holds her ba - by, and she breathes His ho - ly

name. "Je - sus, rest your wea - ry head, close your weep - ing

eyes." As eve - ning falls, she starts to sing a lul - la -

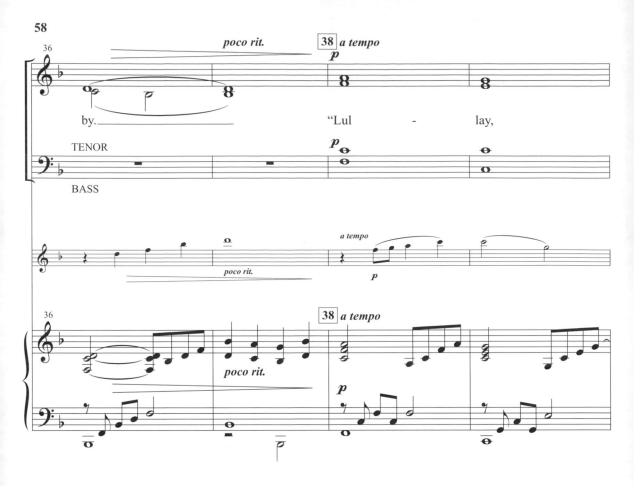

think on gen - tle things."   With lov - ing   arms she holds her

Sav - ior   and she   sings,_____   "Lul -

lay,   lul -   lay,_____   peace__ be

yours__ to - night."

cresc.

f

In the shad - ow of Gol - go - tha, un - der-neath a dark - ened

sky, Ma - ry gent - ly cra - dles Je - sus. Through her tears she

says good - bye._____

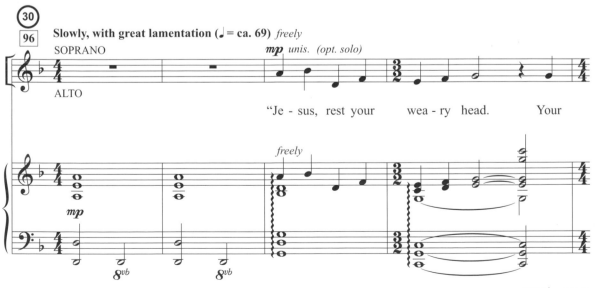

30
96 **Slowly, with great lamentation** (♩ = ca. 69) *freely*

SOPRANO

ALTO

mp unis. (opt. solo)

"Je - sus, rest your   wea - ry head.   Your

peace   be   yours   to - night,

peace   be   yours   to - night,

VIOLIN

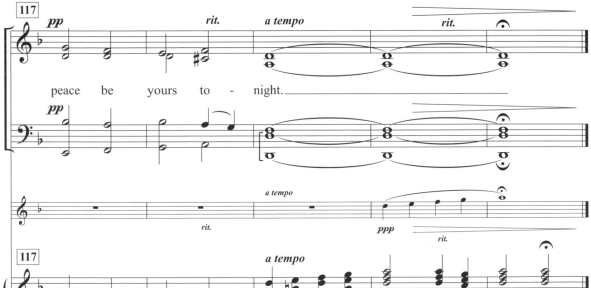

peace   be   yours   to - night.

A PARTING BENEDICTION *[optional]*

And now let us leave this sanctuary of shadows and begin our journey home to the garden. With each step we take, let us carry near our hearts the knowledge of Christ's sacrifice and His unfailing love.

As we make this solemn procession, we will not be afraid, for we remember His promise of peace and we are comforted. We will not walk as people without hope, for joy will come with the morning and the rising Son will restore the garden from a place of death to a paradise of everlasting life.

As we go let us remember Christ wore the crown of thorns and thought of us.

Let us recall His sacred heart was broken and yet He loved us to the end.

With each step we take, let us consider His pierced feet and recall He carried the cross of shame and walked the path of suffering for us.

And as we cling to His nail-scarred hands may we discover our names engraved there…an eternal reminder that we are His children of grace. Amen!

Here are two options for concluding the service following the singing of *Pietà*. These suggestions are optional and you are encouraged to explore other creative ideas to enhance your presentation of the work.

OPTION 1:
The *Epilogue*, is played, during which the congregation files reverently to the altar to touch the cross and extinguish one of the candles. Votive candles and containers of sand may be placed on tables around the sanctuary and/or upon the altar. Each person may take a bit of sand (representing our sin) to extinguish a candle (representing the life of Christ). Each person may take the candle with them as a reminder of Christ's sacrifice on the cross. As the congregants return to their places, the final candles on the altar are extinguished and the celebrant extinguishes the CHRIST candle and speaks the benediction. The celebrant then carries the Christ candle from the sanctuary, followed by the choir, then the narrators, and finally the congregation follows silently until all have left the hall.

OPTION 2:
The Benediction is spoken. The *Epilogue* is then played, during which the congregants silently process to the altar. There they will extinguish candles as described in option 1 after which they will leave the sanctuary leaving behind the lit Christ candle.

EPILOGUE

Music by
JOSEPH M. MARTIN (BMI)

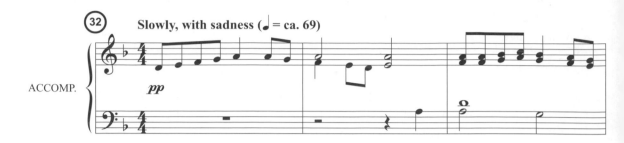

* Tune: PICARDY, French melody, 17th century

Copyright © 2009 by HAL LEONARD - MILWIN MUSIC CORP.
International Copyright Secured. All Rights Reserved.

Duplication of this publication is illegal, and duplication is not granted
by the CCLI, LicenSing or OneLicense.net licenses.

EPILOGUE

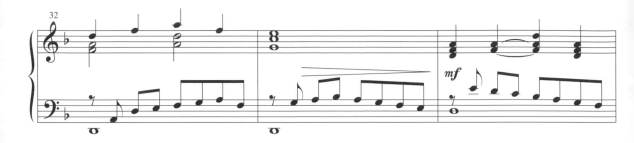

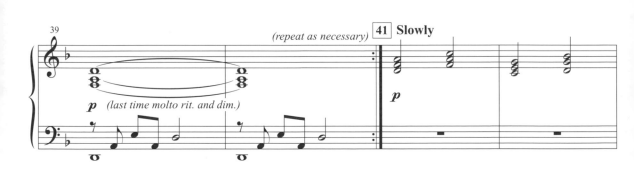

commissioned by Penny Dixon, Director of Music at First Evangelical Lutheran Church
in Idaho Falls, Idaho, in thanksgiving to God for her 35 years of music ministry

PIETÀ

Music by
JOSEPH M. MARTIN (BMI)

VIOLIN (or C-Instrument)

Copyright © 2005, 2009 by HAL LEONARD - MILWIN MUSIC CORP.
International Copyright Secured. All Rights Reserved.

Duplication of this publication is illegal, and duplication is not granted
by the CCLI, LicenSing or OneLicense.net licenses.